Virgo

23 August – 22 September

D1716469

amber
BOOKS

ASTROLOGICAL SIGN DATES:
The precise start and end times for each sign vary by a day or two from year to year as the Gregorian calendar shifts relative to the tropical year. The dates provided in this book are correct for the year 2020.

If you are unsure of the Zodiac sign for your specific birth year, visit: www.yourzodiacsign.com.

Virgo

23 August – 22 September

A guide to understanding yourself, your
friendships and finding your true love

This edition first published in 2020 by
Amber Books Ltd
United House
North Road
London N7 9DP
United Kingdom
www.amberbooks.co.uk
Instagram: amberbooksltd
Facebook: amberbooks
Twitter: @amberbooks

ISBN: 978-1-83886-027-1

Project Editor: Sarah Uttridge
Design: Zoë Mellors

Picture Credits:
All illustrations by Fabbri Publications except the following:
Shutterstock: 20, (owatta), 33 (La Puma), 36 (Slonomysh)

Printed and bound in China

TRADITIONAL CHINESE BOOKBINDING
This book has been produced using traditional Chinese bookbinding
techniques, using a method that was developed during the Ming Dynasty
(1368–1644) and remained in use until the adoption of Western binding
techniques in the early 1900s. In traditional Chinese binding, single sheets
of paper are printed on one side only, and each sheet is folded in half,
with the printed pages on the outside. The book block is then sandwiched
between two boards and sewn together through punched holes close to
the cut edges of the folded sheets.

Contents

Introduction

Virgo

23 August–22 September

Sign: The Virgin

Ruling Planet: Mercury

Gender: Feminine

Element: Earth

Quality: Mutable

Compatibility: Pisces and some Aquarians

Non-compatibility: Leo and Sagittarius

Every man, woman and child is born with a distinct and different destiny. There are no exceptions. Everyone has cosmic significance and a part to play in the life of the universe. This is innate and inescapable, and goes beyond the tiny boundaries of nation, creed and colour.

As we live out our lives on planet Earth, we are, however unknowingly, acting in a greater drama and reacting to impulses that come from distant astronomical bodies, stars and planets millions of light years away. Sceptics pour scorn on the idea that far-distant Saturn, for example, can have any effect on our lives, as the ancient art and science of astrology teaches. But the fact is that we are sparks of energy inhabiting bodies made of the same stuff as the stars, responding like tiny radios to the distant messages they send to Earth.

Each infant carries within it a double blueprint for life: its genetic programming and the pattern of character that comes from the astrological 'clock' that was set in motion at the moment of birth. No one knows the full extent of genetic influence, although it seems to be astonishingly far-reaching, but the power of the horoscope has been well known to the wisest men and women for many centuries.

Our Sun signs provide essential inside information about our destinies. They reveal the secrets of who we really are, and why we are here, laying out before us our potential, the sort of joys and achievements our characteristics may bring about, and warn us of problems to be overcome through the triumph of free will.

Read this book with an open mind and discover who you really are.

The Elements

U p to the beginning of the Age of Enlightenment – the modern scientific era – in the 18th century, it was commonly believed that everything, including human beings, was made up of the four elements: Earth, Air, Fire and Water. These were thought of as the building blocks of life, and each astrological sign had a predominance of one or another. Each created its common characteristics, although too much of any of the elements can produce an unbalanced personality.

Earth Signs

The signs ruled by Earth are Taurus, Virgo and Capricorn. Each manifests the element in different ways. However, in all cases, Earth makes those born under these signs tend to be more practical, sensible and stable than most. They are better 'grounded' or, to put it in another way, they keep their feet on the ground. Whereas others may rush off on madcap schemes or sit around and daydream, those born under Earth signs roll up their sleeves and quietly get on with the job. For example, Arians may be the great explorers and adventurers of the zodiac, but it is Taureans who follow behind, set up camp for them and arrange for provisions to be sent ahead upriver. Taureans are 'the salt of the earth', the plodders who may strike the more dynamic and extrovert signs of the zodiac as being uninspired, but who are invaluable and upright members of society.

Virgoans, always organized, tidy and efficient, are the analysts and notekeepers who keep track of records, accounts and archives so that society knows its history. They are the ones who ensure that the great exploits of the Arian adventurers are known to posterity. Capricornians always have an eye to the future, planning ahead for a rainy day from their lofty mountain peaks, like the Goat that symbolizes their sign. If they are occasionally dour and pessimistic – thanks to the influence of their ruling planet Saturn, who nevertheless encourages them to be disciplined and careful – then they succeed all the more in keeping the wilder excesses of the Fire and Air signs under control.

Earth Signs

Taurus

Virgo

Capricorn

Colours of the Zodiac

Traditionally, each sign of the zodiac has its own colour, which is believed to be 'lucky' or magically empowered for those born under that particular sign. In general, the colours are associated with the ruling planets and are symbolic of their attributes. Many people find that they feel most comfortable when they are wearing their sign's colours, and often choose them without knowing their astrological background.

Virgo

Ruling Planet: Mercury.

Colour: Rich brown and russet reds. These colours anchor the individual to the Earth, balancing the Mercurian potential for flightiness. Many people find brown depressing, however, so it should be used lightly.

The Angelic Hierarchy

A ccording to ancient tradition, each planet is governed by one of the great archangels, who are also rulers of certain aspects of human life. The box below lists the planet that they rule, the areas over which they have influence and their special day of the week.

Raphael

Archangel of Mercury.

Governs: Gemini and Virgo.

Rules: Writing and all forms of communication and learning as well as healing.

Day: Wednesday

The Genders

Traditionally, the twelve signs of the zodiac are divided into Masculine and Feminine, although of course both men and women are born into each.

The characteristics were assigned to the genders aeons ago, well before modern feminism or political correctness, and may now seem old-fashioned to many. However, the signs do seem to be grouped according to the appropriate gender.

The Feminine Signs

The Feminine signs are Taurus, Cancer, Virgo, Scorpio, Capricorn and Pisces. Feminine traits tend to be accentuated in the Water signs Cancer and Pisces.

These signs present gentler, more passive qualities. They are the carers and the nurturers, inclined to take a back seat and worry over the well-being of others. They are artistic and in tune with their intuition, and may be psychic. Self-evidently, these are the motherly and sisterly signs, with all the attendant positive and negative characteristics. They tend to be the power behind the throne, rather than movers and shakers, although many are great achievers, especially in the modern, more egalitarian world, where their qualities are encouraged.

Negatively, the Feminine signs can be fussy, possessive, mean-minded, vindictive, cringing, clinging and over-emotional.

Aquarius, the sign of the coming Age, is endowed with both Masculine and Feminine traits, although it is traditionally categorized as Masculine.

The Ruling Planets

U ntil the 18th century, astrologers knew only the planets of our solar system that could be seen with the naked eye: Mercury, Venus, Mars, Jupiter and Saturn. (For the purposes of astrology, the Sun and the Moon are also counted as planets even though the Sun is a star and the Moon is the satellite of Earth.) Uranus was discovered in 1781, Neptune in 1846 and Pluto was first seen in 1930. Many astrologers believe that the existence of other heavenly bodies – such as the rumoured Vulcan, which hypothetically exists within the orbit of Mercury – is about to be confirmed. Astrologers will then have to agree which signs these 'new' planets will rule, and what human characteristics their discovery will accentuate.

Mercury

Mercury was the name of the Roman messenger god, ruler of communication, whose great energy always kept him on the move. To help him travel fast he had little wings on his ankles and helmet. In Greek mythology he was Hermes, who gave his name to the legendary body of learning known as the Hermetica, which inspired thousands of great names over the centuries, from Leonardo da Vinci to Sir Isaac Newton. Although many scholars once believed that Hermeticism originated with the Greeks, there is increasing evidence that they had merely adapted much older Egyptian wisdom.

The Egyptian version of Mercury was Thoth, god of wisdom, healing and time. Known as 'Thrice-great Thoth', he was worshipped in the form of an ibis-headed man. His secrets were jealously guarded in temples specially dedicated to him in ancient Heliopolis, and passed on only to initiates who had proved worthy of them.

About Mercury

This tiny planet, the nearest to the Sun, is just 4880 km (3000 miles) across, with a year of 88 days – the second-fastest-moving heavenly body after the Moon.

The sacred day of Mercury is Wednesday.

In Scandinavia, the messenger god Loki was also a trickster. So was the Native American Heyeohkah, the mocking version of the creator god, who, nevertheless, showed kindness and compassion to humankind. All the mercurial gods share the same dual nature. They are both trickster and friend of the human race.

Mercury gave his name to quicksilver, the beautiful and unusual liquid metal, which – being a cumulative poison – is also deadly. Mercury proved to be of enduring fascination to generations of alchemists, who sought for centuries to turn this base metal into gold.

Gemini and Virgo are both ruled by Mercury. Typical Geminians are truly mercurial – quick-witted, fast talkers, energetic and volatile. However, there can also be an element of the trickster in them.

Virgoans are great communicators but at a slower pace than Gemini. They think before they speak and can be immensely entertaining, with a highly developed – often self-deprecating – sense of humour.

The modern era, with its unprecedented advances in communication – from the transmission of the first radio signals to the internet – has been an archetypically Mercurial epoch.

The Qualities

I n addition to the influence of gender, the
elements and the planets, each sign of the
zodiac is affected by having an intrinsic quality –
Cardinal, Fixed or Mutable.

Mutable Quality

Those born under the Mutable signs are always
on the move, either physically or mentally, forever
seeking fresh fields and pastures new. They are
restless, versatile and flexible, hating routine and
any form of strict discipline. These individuals can
have butterfly minds, endlessly alighting on new
enthusiasms, fads or crazes, then dropping them just
as quickly and moving on to the next thing. Mutable
people can be unreliable and irresponsible, and
are rarely self-disciplined, although they are often
extremely charming.

Virgo

Excellent communicators, Virgoans make amusing and pleasant companions, revealing a sharp wit and a sense of the absurd. However, their Mutable qualities are tempered by being an Earth sign, which restrains their flights of fancy and makes them essentially realistic. Surprisingly, perhaps, they are not completely put off by change and can adapt very well to new situations and challenges.

Signs and Symbols

Most people are familiar with the zodiac 'zoo' – the collection of symbols that represent the twelve signs. These images reflect the characteristics traditionally assigned to each sign and contain a wealth of knowledge about its true nature.

Each sign of the zodiac is represented by a symbol – the twin fish for Pisces, for example. No one is sure exactly when or why the symbols were chosen, although some authorities believe they date from Sumeria or Mesopotamia, 4000 years before Jesus Christ. The priest-astrologers of the ancient world were the first to impose recognizable patterns on the great constellations – Leo the Lion being one example.

Today, seeing such shapes in the stars may seem fanciful, but thousands of years ago imaginations were more poetic, and many myths told of magical animals, such as the dragon, which had strange powers to influence everyday human life.

Although the ancient Egyptians left few astrological records, they were almost unique in antiquity for worshipping archetypal, animal-headed gods. However, these strange hybrid gods – half-human, half-animal – were worshipped as aspects of one God. Contrary to the general belief that the Egyptians were idolaters, their religion was basically monotheistic. Each statue represented an aspect of the one true God.

Since they were established, the signs have remained unchanged, although there was a movement in the Middle Ages to change the sign of Aquarius to the sign of John the Baptist – presumably because of the connection with water.

The twelve signs of the zodiac do seem particularly apt on the whole, and accurately reflect the archetypal character of Sun sign types. The great Swiss psychoanalyst Carl Gustav Jung (1875–1961) believed that, deep in our psyches, humanity shares a collective unconscious – a set of archetypal images, which, at a profound level, we all understand. The signs of the zodiac form part of this pool of images, conveying eternal truths to our unconscious minds.

Signs and Symbols

Aries

Taurus

Gemini

Cancer

Leo

Virgo

Libra

Scorpio

Sagittarius

Capricorn

Aquarius

Pisces

Virgo The Virgin

The symbol of innocence, the Virgoan sign also, conversely, represents the time of harvest, when the seed sown was finally reaped, a symbol of fertility. This apparent contradiction derives partly from the old confusion of the word 'Virgin' with young woman – the original Greek word for the 'Virgin' Mary in the New Testament simply meant a girl – and partly from associations with pagan goddesses.

All major goddesses who were represented in human form – such as Demeter, Diana, Ceres and Isis – were believed to have three main chronological 'aspects': virgin or young woman, then mother, and finally old woman or crone. These synchronized with, and were symbolized by, the New Moon, the Full Moon, and the Dark of the Moon. However, unlike the Virgin Mary, whose status is unchanging, these goddesses moved fluidly from one aspect to another, thus symbolizing all aspects of womanhood. Some were worshipped in one aspect only – Isis was usually the Mother, for example – but they were understood to be rulers over all female experience, which is why they were so beloved of their women worshippers.

The Sun in Virgo

Sun sign Virgoans are not necessarily virginal,
of course, but they often have the quiet,
unsophisticated air of an inexperienced person,
which can be deceptive. They are meticulous, tidy and
thorough. Typical Sun sign Virgoans keep their own
counsel, and although they are frequently profound
thinkers, they are essentially practical, with few
impossible dreams. These enormously hard-working
people are the first to roll up their sleeves and get on

with the job, while whimsical Geminians or hot-air Arians fail to carry through their grand plans. By contrast, it is the Virgoans who keep records and undertake research to put flesh on the bones of the ambitious projects of others. The Virgoan social style is quiet and unassuming. A typical Virgoan will never interrupt and rarely holds the floor for more than a few minutes. They listen very carefully, however, and when they do voice an opinion, it is often startlingly intelligent, cutting right through to the heart of the matter. Because Virgoans are ruled by Mercury, they are excellent at putting two and two together and seeing connections and inferences others may miss. Their memories are formidable and they can suddenly recall an essential reference from a book they read years ago. This enables them to make the connection with a current project, and the problem is solved. Virgoans are often very witty – with a dry, sometimes surrealistic, sense of humour. They have others in fits of laughter. They can also be brilliant mimics, due to their ability to note quietly every mannerism and characteristic of their subject. And Virgoan jokes linger in the mind longer than most.

Negative Virgoan traits include a capacity for endless worry, which can cloud their own lives

Personality Traits of Virgos

Positive	*Negative*
Meticulous	Worriers
Tidy	Cold
Thorough	Over-analytical
Practical	Obsessed with
Hardworking	routine
Witty	Nagging
Quiet and	Fret about
unassuming	spending
	money

unnecessarily. It also irritates more happy-go-lucky signs. Virgoans can also be naggers, carping about other people's failings and sloppiness. Badly aspected Virgoans can be cold, over-analytical and obsessed with detail. They can become bogged down with trivia, delighting in what others consider boring facts. At work, for example, Virgoans may wax lyrical about new filing systems, and they can be fussy hobbyists, collecting train numbers or matchboxes. They seem obsessed with routines. Everything must always be done in the same way, and in the same order. This type of Virgoan will eat the same food day in and day out, and go to the same holiday spots year after year. They fret about spending money and keep a record of every purchase in tiny, neat handwriting. Everything must be just so, or they can suffer real distress. Virgoans are great for inventing rules on the 'in case' principle. For example, they may insist that no one takes drinks into their study in case some gets spilled onto their computer. It makes sense, but it does not seem to occur to Virgoans that adults can take that risk – most people enjoy a cup of coffee while working at the keyboard. But this is not the extreme type of Virgoan, who hedges his or her life around with a host of rules in order to feel safe.

Appearance

Virgoans have good bone structure and are often highly photogenic. They are attractive, with beautiful eyes that sparkle with intelligence, and can be vain. Their glossy, thick hair frequently rises from a 'widow's peak'. When young, they can seem prematurely old, with a wary, watchful expression. But once in their mid-30s, they seem to look much the same for quite a long time. It is often said that typical Sun sign Virgoans have protruding stomachs, which can be their only rotund feature. However, some types are very angular. Sometimes the first impression they give is of slow, deliberate movements. Curiously, many Virgoans have a slightly unbalanced way of walking, perhaps with a barely perceptible limp. Once animated, though, they can leap into a higher gear, becoming nervy and quick.

Health

All that worry can play havoc with Virgoan digestions. They are often martyrs to their stomachs, and many suffer from Irritable Bowel Syndrome, which greatly embarrasses and inconveniences them. Many also suffer from food

intolerances or full-blown allergies. In this case, they should seek good advice from reputable nutritionists. Usually the only answer to their health problems is to learn to unwind. Yoga or meditation would be good for them. So would going for long walks in the evening and, of course, following a careful diet. Virgoans are particularly sensitive to drugs of all types, whether they are prescribed by their doctor or are herbal concoctions, nicotine or alcohol. In such cases, it is sometimes not enough just to cut down. They may have to abstain completely for the sake of their well-being. Virgoans are notably fussy about their health, and often carry their favourite remedies, vitamins and even their own special brand of mineral water around with them.

The natural life is best for earthy Virgoans. They need plenty of fresh air to blow away the cobwebs and rebalance their energies. Many choose to be vegetarians, which suits their nervy digestions – although they must remember to include a wide variety of foods in their diet, and take extra vitamin B if necessary. Homeopathic and naturopathic remedies often suit Virgoans, and the process of tracking down the right therapies for them appeals to their love of detective work.

Career

Virgoans make excellent nurses because they are practical, calm, disciplined and cheerful. Their quiet confidence and efficiency can be very comforting. They make caring and effective alternative therapists, too, and are often involved in researching their subject in great depth to add to their knowledge. Virgoans also make excellent counsellors or community carers. Some love providing nourishing food for the less fortunate members of society.

Virgoans love making a contribution, and being of service to any group or corporation, to which they will be unfailingly loyal. They are, however, better as members of a team than as bosses. A Virgoan in charge can become nitpicking and hypercritical, forever double-checking the work of others. Untidiness and tardiness are anathema to strongly aspected Virgoans, and they can be intolerant of other ways of doing things. Like their fellow Earth sign, Taurus, they love tradition, convention and rules and regulations for their own sake, even when these are outdated and inefficient. Virgoans like analyzing and collating and are totally at home with columns of figures and computer work. They make superb programmers and are the natural accountants of the zodiac. They can also make highly efficient tax inspectors and private detectives.

Dogged, analytical and intellectual, Virgoans make skilled and inspired research scientists. They rarely let their hearts rule their heads, and some types would show little sentiment towards laboratory animals.

The best careers for Virgos

- Nurse
- Counsellor
- Social worker
- Private detective
- Laboratory technician
- Actor
- Nutritionist
- Accountant

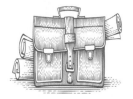

Traditionally associated with the time of harvest, Virgoans are happy planning and cooking meals, and are often found in the catering trade.

Perhaps uncharacteristically, Virgoans, who are normally introverted, can frequently be found in the theatre. They appreciate the chance to cast off their inhibitions and assume another personality on stage. Many actors are actually shy and come to life only when they can hide behind the mask of the character they play. This suits Virgoans completely.

Virgoans have strong opinions, but sometimes hesitate to express them, and often fear attempting something new. They can be excellent business partners, however, even in creative endeavours such as writing or computer graphics, where they will provide the common sense and attention to detail that may escape their more unworldly partners.

Many Virgoans are workaholics, condemning themselves to a life chained to their desk and ignoring the world outside. Relationships, health and opportunities pass them by as they are absorbed in their work. Conversely, there is a type of slothful, unmotivated Virgoan, whose self-worth is too low for them to attempt anything without a fear of failure – so they just do nothing and drift through life.

Relationships

Though they are reliable, responsible, eminently sensible and can be happy in a stable relationship, Virgoans are often very difficult to live with. These fussy, critical people can make life a misery for more relaxed souls by constant complaints about tidiness or anything else. Conversely, there is a very untidy type of Virgoan, who happily lives in apparent chaos, though they usually know, roughly, where the important things are. Curiously, even this type has an element of Virgoan neatness about them – despite the litter. This type is happiest living the single life, with a small circle of like-minded friends who drop in from time to time for a chat. They love surfing the net, which satisfies their craving for accumulating facts and having a vicarious social life at the same time – and all without moving from their chairs.

If they marry, many Virgoans do so more than once, perhaps because they have to learn the hard way all about sharing and tolerance, and because they easily tire of the routine of living with one person. They can be tense in close relationships, which can badly upset their sex lives, and makes it hard for them to become truly intimate with those they love. Some Virgoans prefer others to take the lead sexually, although they soon show an aptitude for experimentation and excitement in bed.

Virgoans can be irritable with those around them, particularly those who are more physical or devil-may-care. They tend to bring their work home, which does not make for jolly family evenings. However, they take their family responsibilities seriously and can be solicitous for the welfare of partners and families. Although careful with money, they can be generous, and usually remember birthdays and anniversaries. Some extreme Virgoans, however, are penny-pinching types who would put the grasping sort of Cancerians to shame, and they may live bleak lives and cause misery to those around them. This extreme type may also invent strange ground rules for those living under the same roof; and they will force them to obey, no matter how inconvenient it may be. This form of control mania arises out of fear of disorder.

Virgoans may find parenthood difficult. The demonstrative motherhood of Cancerians, or the robust fathering of a solid Taurean are not for them. Virgoans find expressing emotion hard, and are often too absorbed in their world of facts, figures and fussing to give much of their time to their youngsters.

It is only when children are capable of rational thought that Virgoan parents truly come into their own, helping their children to learn the rules of life. Later, when the children are on the verge of independence and young adulthood, Virgoan parents are more than happy to help with finances, find a suitable mortgage, explain the intricacies of pensions and insurance schemes and scrutinize the small print of any financial or contractual agreement. They can make far better grandparents than parents. By that time of life, they may well have learned to relax and to enjoy the spontaneity of having very young children around them.

Ideal Partner

Virgoans can find close relationships a trial. But if near opposites attract, they will go for deep, dark Scorpians, whose intensity adds colour to their more plodding lives, and whose sexuality can encourage them to lose their inhibitions. Gentle Pisceans, with their soft emotions, can make Virgoans realize that they can relax and enjoy home life. Some types of Aquarian also bring out the best in Virgo, and madcap Arians can bring a totally different energy into their lives. Here, the relationship may be too fiery to survive, but it will be fun while it lasts. Leos, with their love of display, can help Virgoans to discover the joy and laughter they find so elusive. Although their extravagance can worry some Virgoans, more relaxed ones can fare well with Leos.

Like fellow Venusians of the bovine sort, gentle Virgoans can be disconcerted by banner-waving Aquarians; although they may enjoy deep discussions with them. The energy and innocence of a Sagittarian may be initially appealing, but the Sagittarian lifestyle is ultimately too unpredictable.

Compatibility in Relationships

Aries
20 March–19 April

Quick-fire Arians have a certain allure for more timid Virgoans but prove too combustible in the long term.

Capricorn
21 December–20 January

Virgoans appreciate the Goat's measured approach to life and love, but even they need more adventurousness.

Cancer
21 June–21 July

Loving, sympathetic Cancerians can hit it off with sensible Virgoans, but they will cause too many scenes.

Taurus
20 April–20 May

Both being Earth signs, they understand each other well, but life can lack that all-important spark.

Libra
23 September–22 October

Romantic, sensitive Librans can make amenable partners for Virgoans, but they may lack staying power.

Leo
22 July–22 August

Virgoans may love to bask in reflected Leonine glory, but can find Leo's overbearing manner ultimately offputting.

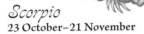

Scorpio
23 October–21 November

Though attracted sexually, straightforward Virgoans are scared off by the Scorpian's sharp tongue.

Virgo
23 August–22 September

Though safe, this can be a deeply dull combination. Two Virgoans will rarely have a sparkling love life.

Aquarius
21 January–18 February

Virgoans often admire Aquarians greatly, but their lifestyles are too divergent for lasting bonds to develop.

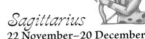

Sagittarius
22 November–20 December

True Virgoans are often horrified by Sagittarian fecklessness and their capacity to live in the moment.

Gemini
21 May–20 June

They will enjoy each other's company, but frivolous and flighty Geminians can frighten Virgoans away.

Pisces
19 February–19 March

Something about loving, needy Pisceans can bring out the best in the more supportive, well-grounded Virgoan.

The Virgoan Child

Always fretting and worrying, Virgoan children need to have their self-esteem constantly reinforced. They need to be told they can succeed, and encouraged to be adventurous. Otherwise, they will simply become increasingly timorous and insecure. They need to have their expectations notched up, to be told time and time again that it is a good idea to aim for the top, to have dreams and goals and to fight for them. Equally, however, goal-setting should be realistic, or they will see through it and never make any attempt at rising to the challenge. The best thing to do is to encourage them to go for gold in their chosen field, or a subject that is close to Virgoan hearts, rather than forcing them to compete in unappealing subjects. This might include taking part in the school play, or joining a team sport – they can also be extremely loyal team supporters – or helping in an administrative capacity with special interest clubs or charities.

Virgoans are neat, tidy children on the whole. They may not present the most creative or promising work, but it will always be legible and clean. They do have a lazy streak, though, but prefer to be kept busy at some clearly defined task where they can see they are making progress. They like being told what to do, rather than taking the initiative; although they should be actively encouraged to think for themselves, perhaps through puzzles and quiz games. They are better at slow, steady coursework and do not usually shine when it comes to sitting examinations.

They can often be found deeply absorbed in the local library, while more boisterous children are kicking a ball around. Because they tend to be tidy, do their homework on time and dislike danger, upheaval or anything that disrupts their normal routine, others may think of them as prigs. Sometimes they are, but in reality they just like a quiet life – making small steps for man rather than giant leaps for mankind.

Famous Virgoans

Queen Elizabeth I

Greta Garbo

Peter Sellers

Jesse James

B.B. King

Agatha Christie

Sean Connery

Stephen King

Prince Albert

Yasser Arafat

Lauren Bacall

Anton Bruckner

Edgar Rice Burroughs

John Cage

Maurice Chevalier

Antonin Dvorak

Gustav Holst

H.G. Wells

Mary Shelley

Aristotle Onassis

Finding Your Sun Sign (2020 dates)

Aries	20 March–19 April*
Taurus	20 April–20 May
Gemini	21 May–20 June
Cancer	21 June–21 July
Leo	22 July–22 August
Virgo	23 August–22 September
Libra	23 September–22 October
Scorpio	23 October–21 November
Sagittarius	22 November–20 December
Capricorn	21 December–20 January
Aquarius	21 January–18 February
Pisces	19 February–19 March

*The dates provided in this book reflect the year 2020.
Dates may vary by a day or two from year to year.